Embroidery

Written by
Judy Ann Sadler

Illustrated by
June Bradford

KIDS CAN PRESS

To "the outlaws" — Greg, Harriet, Bill, Steve, Joseph, Melanie, Carolynn and Paul — who have embroidered our lives with their laughter, generosity, warmth and love.

Text © 2004 Judy Ann Sadler
Illustrations © 2004 June Bradford

KIDS CAN DO IT and the 📖 logo are trademarks of Kids Can Press Ltd.

Kids Can Press acknowledges the financial support of the Government of Ontario, through the Ontario Media Development Corporation's Ontario Book Initiative, and the Government of Canada, through the BPIDP, for our publishing activity.

Published in Canada by
Kids Can Press Ltd.
29 Birch Avenue
Toronto, ON M4V 1E2

Published in the U.S. by
Kids Can Press Ltd.
2250 Military Road
Tonawanda, NY 14150

www.kidscanpress.com

Edited by Alice Rowe
Designed by Karen Powers
Photography by Frank Baldassarra
Printed in Hong Kong, China, by Wing King Tong

The hardcover edition of this book is smyth sewn casebound.
The paperback edition of this book is limp sewn with a drawn-on cover.

CM 04 0 9 8 7 6 5 4 3 2 1
CM PA 04 0 9 8 7 6 5 4 3 2 1

National Library of Canada Cataloguing in Publication Data

Sadler, Judy Ann, 1959–
Embroidery / written by Judy Ann Sadler ; illustrated by June Bradford.

(Kids can do it)

ISBN 1-55337-616-1 (bound). ISBN 1-55337-617-X (pbk.)

1. Embroidery — Juvenile literature. I. Bradford, June II. Title. III. Series.

TT770.5.S23 2004   j746.44   C2003-903377-5

Kids Can Press is a **corus**™ Entertainment company

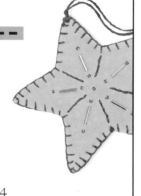

Contents

Introduction

Embroidery is like drawing with a needle and thread. Just about any design you can imagine can be stitched onto paper, fabric or clothing. There are hundreds of embroidery stitches, but you need to know only a few to create some amazing designs. In this book, you will find all the instructions you need to make many neat projects as well as ideas for personalizing and decorating your clothes.

Make a colorful patterned bracelet, a ladybug fridge magnet, a cozy fleece blanket and a handy decorated CD pouch. Embroider snowflakes on your hat or stars on your jacket. Make neat stuff for yourself and cards and gifts for family and friends. Once you start, you'll want to embroider everything. Happy stitching!

MATERIALS

Fabric

You can embroider almost any fabric including clothing. Even-weave fabrics are especially made for embroidery. These fabrics have the same number of threads in each direction, making it easy to sew evenly spaced stitches that are all the same size. The cross-stitch projects tell you to use Aida cloth, an even-weave fabric that has holes showing you where to stitch. It is available in different counts (squares per inch) at craft supply stores. When the instructions refer to the right side of the fabric, this means the good side, the outside or the side that shows on your finished project. Some fabrics, such as felt, fleece, plain and even-weave fabrics, don't have right and wrong sides.

Thread

You can use many types of thread and yarn for embroidery, but for most of these projects, you will need six-strand cotton embroidery floss. Skeins of floss come in hundreds of dazzling colors. Make sure you use high-quality colorfast floss. Colorfast means that the color won't run or fade when the embroidery is washed. You can use the six strands together or divide them or mix them with strands of other colors.

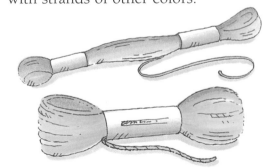

Needles

For most embroidery, use a needle with a sharp point that's called an embroidery or crewel needle. When you embroider even-weave fabrics such as Aida cloth, use a tapestry needle. Tapestry needles have blunt tips that don't split the threads in the fabric as you stitch, but pass between them instead. When you are embroidering with yarn or all six strands of embroidery floss, or working on thick fabrics such as denim and fleece, use a chenille needle. It is a sturdy needle with a large eye and sharp point. To add beads to your embroidery, you may need a long, thin beading needle. For regular hand sewing, you can use an embroidery needle or a type of sewing needle called a sharp. Needles may rust, so never leave a needle stuck in the fabric you are embroidering.

Embroidery hoops

For many projects, you will need an embroidery hoop (also called a ring frame). Usually made of wood or plastic, a hoop holds your fabric taut as you stitch. This helps keep your stitches even and the finished embroidery smooth. A hoop is made of two pieces: an inner ring and a split outer ring with a screw closure. The screw lets you adjust the size of the outer ring for thick or thin fabric. It's a good idea to have a small hoop about 8 cm (3 in.) in diameter and a large hoop about 15 cm (6 in.) in diameter.

Fabric markers

Draw or transfer your designs onto fabric with a water-erasable fabric marker (the marks disappear when you dab water on them), a sharp pencil, dressmaker's tracing paper or a chalk pencil.

Scissors

Use small, sharp scissors for snipping threads and large, sharp scissors for cutting fabric. Pinking shears cut a zigzag edge, which prevents fabric from fraying.

Straight pins

It's a good idea to use straight pins with beads on the ends, called glass head pins. They are comfortable to hold and easy to find if you drop one. Handle pins carefully and store them in a pincushion (page 14) or small container.

Other stuff

You may need beads, buttons, cord or ribbon, cardboard, card stock (heavy paper), a large safety pin, a seam ripper, Velcro, masking tape, a magnet and white craft glue for some projects. You may also need a bit of polyester fiber stuffing, but if you don't have any, use clean, cut-up cloth or panty hose, or cotton balls or batting.

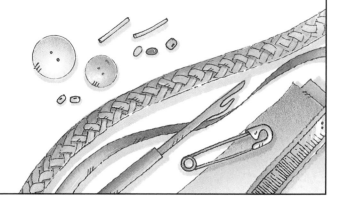

Getting ready to embroider

HANDLING EMBROIDERY FLOSS

A skein of embroidery floss usually has two small bands around it. These labels show the brand name, fiber content and length. One label also has a color number on it. Many embroidery patterns recommend certain color numbers, so be sure to keep the labels together with their floss.

When you need some floss, find the end or "tail" at one end of the skein. Hold the skein lightly at the other end while you slowly pull out the tail. Cut off about 50 cm (20 in.).

There are six strands in the floss. If you need to divide them (the instructions for each project tell you how many strands to use), untwist about 2.5 cm (1 in.) at one end, and separate the number of strands you need. Hold the separated strands and the other strands slightly apart in one hand and let the length of floss hang freely. Very slowly run the thumb of your other hand down the floss between the divided groups, allowing the strands to untwist and separate.

Keep your floss collection tidy and untangled by storing each skein, along with leftover strands (wind them around short strips of cardboard), in a snack-sized plastic bag. To quickly find the right color, tape the skein band or write the color number on the bag.

USING AN EMBROIDERY HOOP

Unscrew the outside hoop to separate the two rings. Lay the inner ring flat on the table, then place the fabric over it, right side up, so that your pattern is centered. Slide the outer ring down over the inner ring so the fabric is sandwiched between the two rings. Begin to tighten the screw, then gently pull the fabric edges until the fabric is smooth. Tighten the screw. When you set aside your embroidery, always remove the fabric from the hoop. If the hoop leaves ridges on your finished embroidery, ask an adult to help you gently iron it, wrong side up, using a low-heat setting.

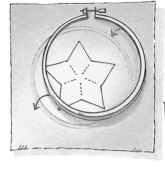

TRANSFERRING A PATTERN

Whenever the project instructions say to transfer the pattern onto fabric or clothing, refer to this page for a few easy ways. The supplies are available at fabric and craft supply stores. You will find many wonderful patterns in this book, but you can also check out magazines, photographs, your own drawings and the world around you. If you are using your own design, you can reduce or enlarge it on a photocopier.

Tracing on a window

Use this method with thin or light-colored fabrics such as Aida cloth, medium-weight cotton and thin, light-colored felt. Begin by retracing the pattern with a black permanent marker. Tape the paper pattern to a brightly lit window. Center the fabric, right side facing you, on the pattern and tape it on, too. With a water-erasable fabric marker, sharp pencil or chalk pencil, trace the pattern onto the fabric.

Dressmaker's tracing paper

Use light-colored tracing paper for dark fabric and dark-colored paper for light fabric. Tape your fabric, right side up, to a smooth, hard surface. Center the paper pattern, right side up, on the fabric and tape down only the top corners. Slide the dressmaker's tracing paper, carbon-side down, between the fabric and the pattern. Smooth all three layers, then tape down the bottom corners of the pattern. Firmly trace the pattern with a pencil or dry ballpoint pen. Carefully peel off the tape at one corner and lift the tracing paper to see if you pressed hard enough. If not, carefully smooth the layers, re-tape the corner and retrace any faint lines.

Drawing

Use a water-erasable fabric marker, sharp pencil or chalk pencil to draw a design directly onto your fabric. Practice drawing the design on paper first.

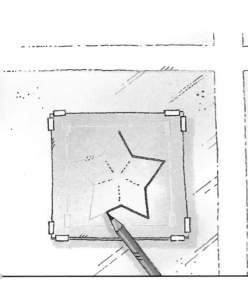

Embroidery stitches

Refer to these pages for all the information you need to start stitching.

THREADING A NEEDLE

Cut a 50 cm (20 in.) length of embroidery floss, thread or yarn. Moisten one end in your mouth, pinch it together and thread it through the eye of the needle.

Or use a needle threader by poking the wire loop through the eye of the needle, threading the floss through the wire loop, then pulling the wire and floss back through the eye.

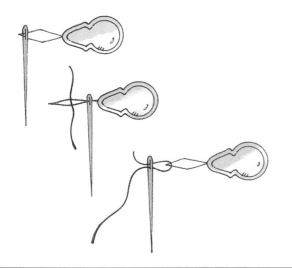

BEGINNING AND ENDING YOUR STITCHING

To make a knot, lick your index finger and wind the longer thread end around it once. (If the instructions call for doubled thread, make sure the ends are even, then wind both ends around your index finger.) With your thumb, roll the thread off your finger and pull to make a knot.

When you run out of thread or reach the end of your stitching, make two or three small stitches over or near the last stitch. Make a small loop on the wrong side of the fabric and bring your needle through it. With the tip of your needle, hold the loop close to the fabric, then tighten the knot. Trim the leftover thread or floss.

For the cross-stitch projects, leave a 10 cm (4 in.) tail at the beginning of your work. After you've made some stitches, thread the tail through a needle and weave the tail back and forth under the stitches on the wrong side of the fabric. When you reach the end of your floss or stitching, weave the floss under the stitches on the wrong side of the fabric. Trim the leftover floss.

BACKSTITCH

Use this stitch with embroidery floss to create decorative stitching and, with regular thread, to sew fabric together. If you have a sewing machine, you can ask an adult to help you use the machine straight stitch when the instructions call for backstitching to sew fabric together.

1. With knotted embroidery floss or thread in your needle, push the needle up through the fabric about 0.5 cm (¼ in.) in from where you want the stitch line to start and make a small stitch backward.

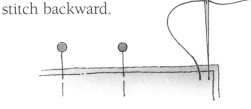

2. Push the needle up through the fabric a little way in front of the first stitch.

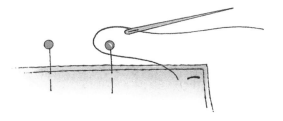

3. Push the needle down through the fabric where it first came up. Keep stitching in this way, making the stitches small and even.

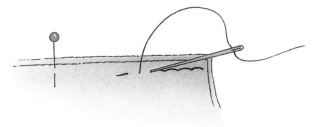

OVERCAST STITCH

Use this stitch along your fabric's raw (unfinished) edges. If you have a sewing machine, you can ask an adult to help you use the machine zigzag stitch when the instructions call for overcast stitching.

1. With knotted thread in your needle, push the needle up through the fabric.

2. Bring the needle around the edge of the fabric and push it up through the fabric a little way along from the first stitch. Keep stitching in this way.

RUNNING STITCH

1. With knotted floss in your needle, push the needle up through the fabric.

2. Push the needle down through the fabric a little way along from where it just came up. Keep stitching in this way, making the stitches and spaces the same length.

DECORATED RUNNING STITCH

Here are some neat ways to jazz up the running stitch.

After you've finished a row of running stitches, use a tapestry needle to wind a different color of embroidery floss from right to left under each stitch.

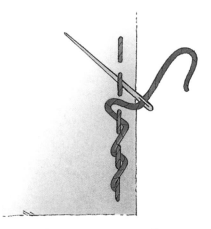

You can also use the tapestry needle to lace a contrasting color of floss up through one stitch, down through the next, and so on.

Use a third color of floss to lace in the opposite direction.

BLANKET STITCH

1. With knotted embroidery floss in your needle, push the needle up through the fabric.

2. Push the needle down through the fabric about 1 cm (½ in.) from where the needle came up. Loop the floss behind the needle as you pull it through the fabric. This first stitch will be slanted.

3. Push the needle back down through the fabric. Keep stitching in this way.

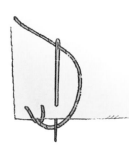

4. When you get back to where you started, push the needle under the first stitch loop, straighten it, then anchor it with a tiny stitch at the edge of the fabric.

SATIN STITCH

Use this stitch to fill in small areas with color.

1. With knotted embroidery floss in your needle, push the needle up through the fabric at one edge of the pattern. Push it back down at the other edge, straight across from where the needle came up.

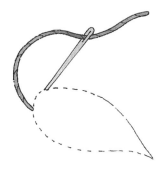

2. Push the needle back up right beside the first stitch and then back down straight across from where the needle came up. Keep stitching in this way until the area is filled in. The stitches should be so close together that no fabric shows through, and the edges should be smooth.

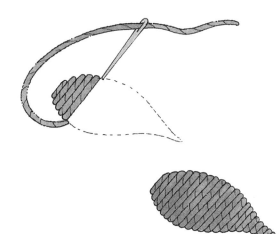

STRAIGHT STITCH

Make a single satin stitch and you've made a straight stitch. You can make straight stitches of different lengths and in any direction.

LONG-AND-SHORT STITCH

Use this stitch to fill in large areas.

1. With knotted embroidery floss in your needle, make one long, then one short satin stitch (see above) along one edge of the pattern.

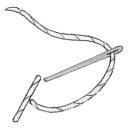

2. Use satin stitches of equal length in the rest of the rows to fill in the area.

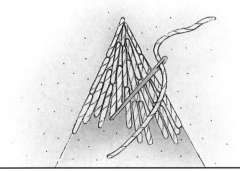

CLOUD-FILLING STITCH

Fill in spaces and create neat patterns with this stitch. You can stitch in rows or in a circle.

1. With knotted embroidery floss in your needle, stitch an evenly spaced row of short, vertical straight stitches (page 11).

2. Below the first row, stitch a second row so that the stitches are centered between the stitches in the first row.

3. Stitch a third row directly below the stitches in the first row.

4. Use a tapestry needle to weave a different color of embroidery floss back and forth between the first and second rows, then between the second and third rows.

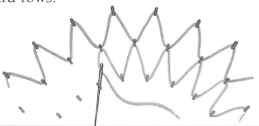

FRENCH KNOT

For the first French knot you make with each length of embroidery floss, you will need to make a knot in the end of your floss.

1. With one hand, push the needle up through the fabric where you want to make the knot.

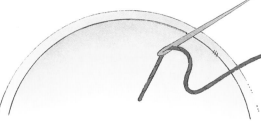

2. Holding the floss between the index finger and thumb of your other hand, wrap the floss around the needle three times.

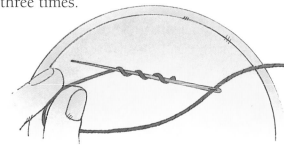

3. Push the needle down through the fabric right beside where it came up. Keep the floss wrapped tightly around the needle as you pull it through so that the knot holds its shape.

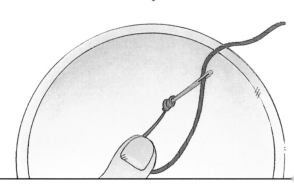

CHAIN STITCH

1. With knotted embroidery floss in your needle, push the needle up through the fabric. Holding a loop of floss with your thumb, push the tip of the needle down through the fabric where it came up.

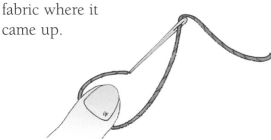

2. Push the needle back up through the fabric a little way over, inside the loop, and hold the loop under the needle as you pull the needle up through the fabric. Gently tighten the loop.

3. Push the needle down through the fabric where it just came up. Keep stitching in this way to form a chain.

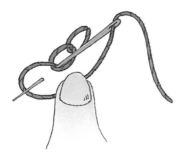

LAZY-DAISY STITCH

Follow steps 1 and 2 for the chain stitch, then, just outside the loop, push the needle down through the fabric.

To make a flower, stitch a circle of lazy-daisy stitches.

Flower pincushion

This fun, easy-to-make pincushion is a handy place to keep your needles and pins.

YOU WILL NEED

- two 13 cm (5 in.) different-colored squares of felt
- embroidery floss and an embroidery needle
- stuffing (page 5)
- a pencil, paper, scissors, pins

1 Trace the flower and flower-center patterns onto paper. Cut them out.

2 Trace each pattern onto a different color of felt and cut them out.

3 With three strands of embroidery floss, blanket-stitch (page 10) all around the edge of the flower.

4 Pin the flower center to the flower. With three strands of floss, use a running stitch (page 9) to sew the center to the flower, leaving a small opening for the stuffing. Remove the pins as you sew.

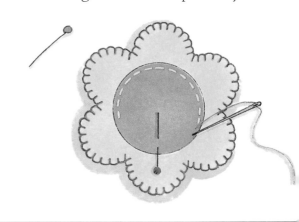

5 Firmly stuff the center and stitch the opening closed.

Instead of blanket-stitching the flower edge, make French knots all around the edge.

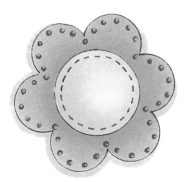

With a beading needle and thread to match your felt, sew beads around the flower center.

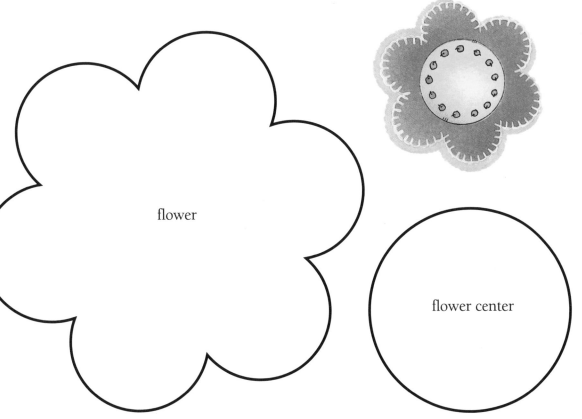

flower

flower center

Stitched greeting card

Many colors of card stock are available at art supply stores and print shops.

YOU WILL NEED

- a piece of card stock or heavy paper about 22 cm x 14 cm (8 1/2 in. x 5 1/2 in.)
- corrugated cardboard • 2 paper clips
- embroidery floss and a tapestry needle
- clear tape or white craft glue
- a pencil, paper, scissors, a pushpin, crayons, pencil crayons or markers

1 Fold the card stock in half so the short ends are even.

2 Trace one of the patterns onto paper or draw your own design to fit on the front of the card. Try a face, flowers, an animal or words.

3 Unfold the card and place it, face up, on the cardboard. Center your pattern on the front of the card and paper-clip it in place.

4 With the pushpin, poke holes along the outline of the pattern. Make sure you poke through the paper and card stock into the cardboard. Remove the pattern.

5 With three strands of embroidery floss, backstitch (page 9) the outline on the card, sewing through the holes. Add beads and other stitches such as French knots (page 12) to make your card unique.

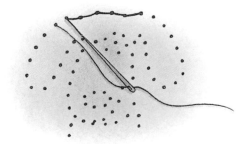

6 On the inside front of the card, center and glue or tape on a piece of paper. Sign and date the back of the card.

OTHER IDEAS

Embroider flowers all over the front of your card using lazy-daisy stitches (page 13).

Beaded star ornament

Make this pretty star-shaped ornament for a drawer pull, doorknob or tree.

1 Trace the star with embroidery pattern (page 20) onto paper. Transfer it (page 7) onto the center of one felt square. Set aside the other felt square.

2 Place the felt in the hoop (page 6) so the star is centered. With three strands of embroidery floss, backstitch (page 9) the embroidery lines.

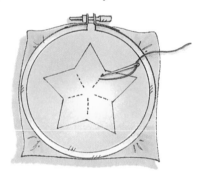

3 With knotted thread in a beading needle, push the needle up through the felt between two stitched lines. Thread on a seed bead. Push the needle down through the felt right beside where it came up to fasten it in place.

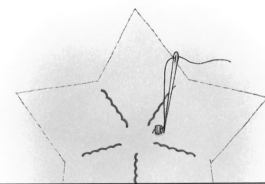

4 Push the needle back up through the felt a little way out. Thread on a bugle bead and push the needle down through the felt at the end of the bead to fasten it in place.

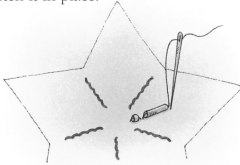

5 Push the needle up through the felt a little way out. Thread on a second seed bead and fasten it in place.

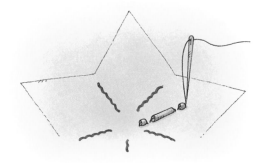

6 Keep stitching in this way to sew beads between all the stitched lines. Finish by stitching a seed bead at the center. Knot the thread on the wrong side and trim it.

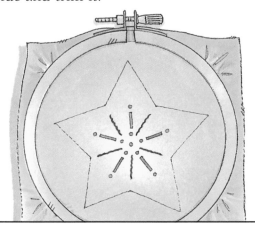

7 Remove the hoop. Cut out the star and trace it onto the other felt square. Cut out the second star.

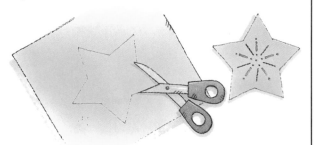

8 Line up the stars and pin them together, beaded side up. With three strands of floss, blanket-stitch (page 10) or overcast-stitch (page 9) them together, leaving a small opening for the stuffing. Remove the pins as you sew.

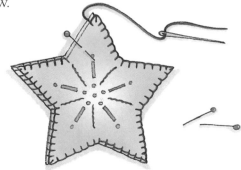

9 Use closed scissors to gently poke stuffing into the points of the star. Stuff the center and stitch the opening closed.

Instructions continue on the next page ☞

10 To make a loop, thread all six strands of a 20 cm (8 in.) length of floss (you could try metallic floss) through a chenille needle. Push the needle through the star's top point. Remove the needle, pull the floss so the ends are even and tie them together with one overhand knot at the point and one at the ends. If you like, you can tie a ribbon into a bow around the base of the loop.

OTHER IDEAS

For extra sparkle, sew a bead or dab glitter glue on each point of the star.

To create a garland, make three or more stars. With small stitches, sew them together, point to point.

star with embroidery pattern

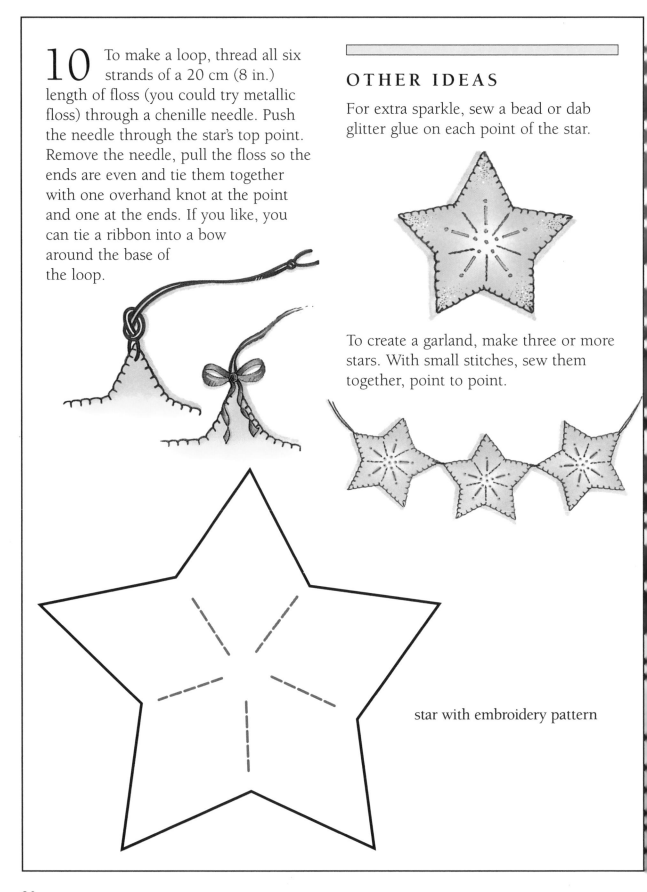

CD pouch

Carry up to five CDs in their cases or use this pouch as a small purse.

YOU WILL NEED

- two 23 cm (9 in.) squares of sturdy fabric
- a sewing needle and thread to match your fabric
- pinking shears (optional)
- supplies for transferring a pattern (page 7)
- a large embroidery hoop
- embroidery floss, an embroidery needle and a tapestry needle
- a 15 cm (6 in.) strip of narrow Velcro
- a hot-glue gun (optional)
- a 125 cm (50 in.) length of cord
- a pencil, paper, scissors, pins, a ruler, an iron

1 To prevent the fabric squares from fraying, overcast-stitch (page 9) the edges with a sewing needle and thread, or trim them with pinking shears.

2 Trace the pattern (page 23) onto paper. Transfer it (page 7) onto the center of the right side of one fabric square.

3 Place the square in the embroidery hoop (page 6). With three strands of embroidery floss, straight-stitch (page 11) the starburst in the center, then straight-stitch the circle of Xs around the starburst.

4 French-knot (page 12) each dot on the next circle and just beyond each point of the starburst.

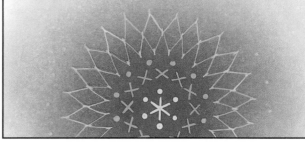

Instructions continue on the next page ☞

5 Use the cloud-filling stitch (page 12) to embroider the next three circles. Use the same color or three different colors.

6 Finish with another circle of French knots.

7 Remove the hoop. If you like, embroider the other square with the same pattern or your own design.

8 With the right sides together, pin the squares along three edges.

9 With a sewing needle and thread, backstitch (page 9) about 1 cm (½ in.) in from the pinned edges. Remove the pins as you sew.

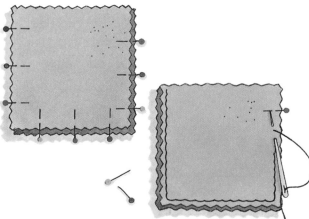

10 Ask an adult to help you fold over, press and pin 1 cm (½ in.) around the top edge. With two strands of floss, backstitch or blanket-stitch (page 10) the hem. Remove the pins as you sew.

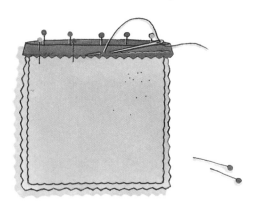

11 Open and refold each bottom corner so the bottom and side seams are together. From each corner, measure 4 cm (1 ½ in.) along each fold and mark with a pin. Backstitch across each corner from pin to pin. Remove the pins and turn the pouch right side out.

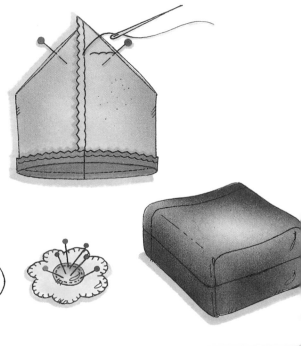

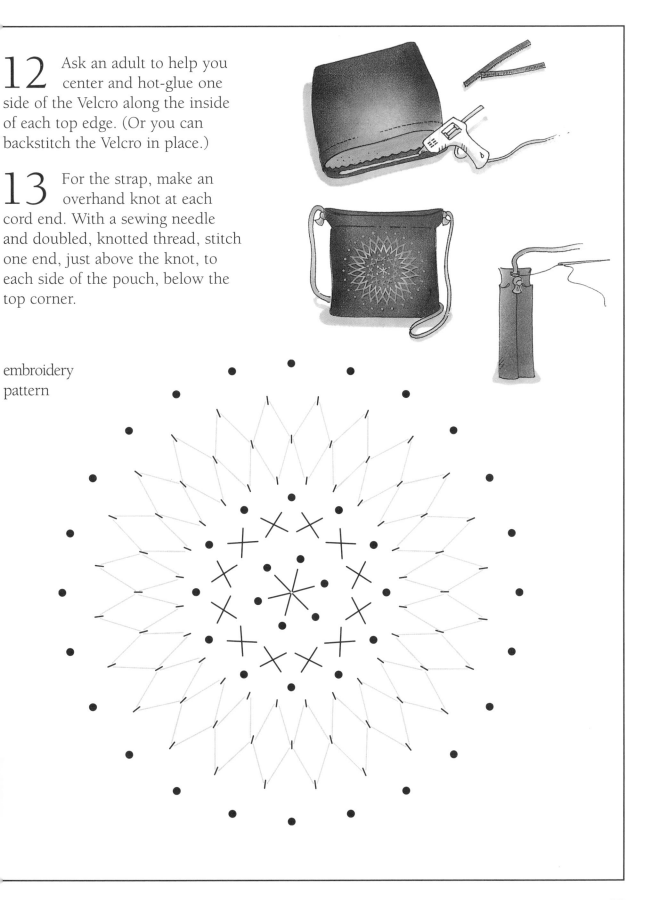

12 Ask an adult to help you center and hot-glue one side of the Velcro along the inside of each top edge. (Or you can backstitch the Velcro in place.)

13 For the strap, make an overhand knot at each cord end. With a sewing needle and doubled, knotted thread, stitch one end, just above the knot, to each side of the pouch, below the top corner.

embroidery
pattern

Drawstring bag

Use this embroidered bag to tote books, shoes or your latest embroidery project.

YOU WILL NEED

- a piece of fabric about 90 cm x 45 cm (36 in. x 18 in.)
- a sewing needle and thread to match your fabric
- a small embroidery hoop
- pinking shears (optional)
- embroidery floss and an embroidery needle
- an assortment of buttons
- 2 m (2 yd.) of heavy cord or ribbon
- white craft glue or clear nail polish (optional)
- a pencil, paper, scissors, pins, a ruler, a large safety pin, an iron

1 To prevent the fabric from fraying, overcast-stitch (page 9) the edges with a sewing needle and thread, or trim them with pinking shears.

2 Place the fabric in the hoop (page 6). With six strands of embroidery floss, push the needle up through the fabric (avoid stitching within 5 cm/2 in. of the fabric edges) and through a hole in a button. Push the needle down through the other holes then knot the floss. Stitch on four-hole buttons in an **X** pattern.

3 With six strands of floss, lazy-daisy-stitch (page 13), French-knot (page 12), backstitch (page 9) or satin-stitch (page 11) petals around the button. Keep sewing on as many buttons as you like and embroidering petals in this way. Remove the hoop.

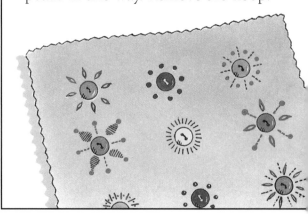

4 Fold the fabric in half, wrong side out, so the short top edges are even. Pin along the two side edges. With a sewing needle and thread, backstitch 1 cm (½ in.) in from the pinned edges. Remove the pins as you sew.

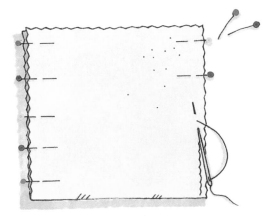

5 Ask an adult to help you fold over, press and pin 3 cm (1¼ in.) around the top edge. With three strands of floss or a sewing needle and thread, backstitch the hem to make a casing for the cord. Remove the pins as you sew. Turn the bag right side out.

6 With scissors or a seam ripper, carefully cut the stitches on the inside and outside of the casing at each side seam. With a sewing needle and thread, make a few stitches below the opening on the inside and outside.

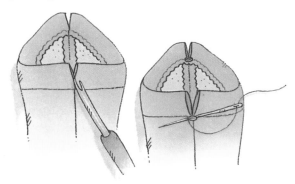

7 Cut the cord in half. Fasten the safety pin to one half. Beginning and ending at the right side seam, thread the cord through the casing. Remove the pin and tie the cord ends together with an overhand knot.

8 Beginning and ending at the left side seam, thread the other cord through the casing. Remove the pin and knot the cord ends. If the ends fray, dab them with a little glue or clear nail polish.

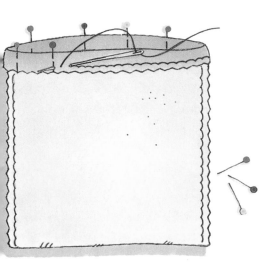

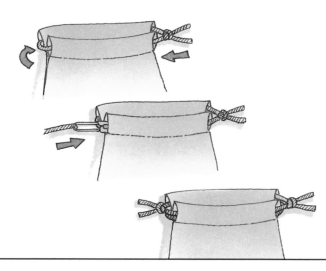

Embroidered clothing

Make your clothing a work of art.
Use a pattern from these pages or
other pages in this book, or
draw your own design.

1 Before you begin, wash and dry the clothing — new or old.

2 Ask an adult to help you press it (unless it's synthetic fleece).

3 Lay it flat, right side up, on a table and tape it down (it may be helpful to slide a piece of cardboard between the layers).

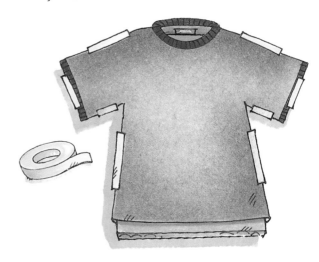

4 Check the instructions for each project, then transfer (page 7) the pattern or draw your own design. Remove the tape and cardboard.

5 Follow the stitching instructions for each item of clothing.

Remember these tips:

- For a stretchy item of clothing, such as a T-shirt or sweatshirt, be careful not to stretch it out of shape in the hoop.

- For jeans and jackets, if the fabric is doubled or too thick to fit in a hoop, work without one. Be careful not to pull the stitches tight or the clothing will pucker.

- For hats, gloves, mittens, socks and shoes, place one hand inside the garment as you stitch to make sure you are embroidering only one layer.

Hat and scarf

LET IT SNOW!

Using the snowflake patterns as guides, use a fabric marker (page 5) to draw different-sized snowflakes onto a hat, scarf and, if you like, mittens, too.

With a chenille needle and yarn or six strands of embroidery floss, backstitch (page 9) the snowflakes.

OTHER IDEAS

To make a scarf, cut a strip of fleece about 140 cm x 30 cm (56 in. x 12 in.). To add a fringe, cut slits, 8 cm (3 in.) deep, about 1 cm (½ in.) apart along each end.

snowflakes

27

Jacket

SEEING STARS

Position and transfer the small star pattern (below) over each buttonhole on the front. With six strands of a different color of embroidery floss for each star, backstitch (page 9) the outlines. If you like, use three strands of floss and the long-and-short stitch (page 11) to fill them in. You can also stitch small stars along the cuffs, collar or pockets.

Transfer the outline only of the large star pattern (page 20) onto one shoulder. With six strands of floss, backstitch the star outline and the heartstring. With six strands of floss, stitch French knots (page 12) along the heart outline. With three strands of floss, fill in small sections of the star with satin stitch (page 11) and large sections with the long-and-short stitch. With six strands of floss, French-knot just beyond each point of the star and anywhere else you like.

small star

Jeans

ROW ON ROW

With a ruler and fabric marker (page 5), mark lines about 1 cm (½ in.) apart around the hems of your jeans. With six strands of a different color of embroidery floss for each line, embroider a different stitch (pages 9 to 13) along each line.

Fleece blanket

These instructions are for a cozy, wrap-yourself-up-sized blanket, but you can make this blanket any size you like.

YOU WILL NEED

- 150 cm (60 in.) square of synthetic fleece
- embroidery floss and a large embroidery needle, or yarn and a chenille needle
- scraps of different colors of fleece, including green
- a fabric marker (page 5)
- a pencil, paper, scissors, pins, thin cardboard, a glue stick

1 Trim any ragged or crooked edges of the fleece and round the corners.

2 With an embroidery needle and six strands of embroidery floss or a chenille needle and yarn, blanket-stitch (page 10) the blanket edges.

3 Trace the flower pattern (page 15), and the leaf and small flower-center patterns (page 31) onto paper. Cut them out, glue them onto cardboard and cut them out.

4 With a fabric marker, trace the cardboard flower and flower-center patterns eight times each onto different colors of fleece. Trace the leaf pattern 16 times onto the green fleece. Cut them out.

5 With three strands of floss, blanket-stitch a center to each flower.

6 Arrange and pin one or three flowers in each corner of the blanket, tucking one to three leaves under the edge of each flower.

7 With six strands of floss, sew the flowers and leaves to the blanket: Sew a long straight stitch (page 11) to divide the flower petals. Sew two long straight stitches in a **V** shape to make each leaf vein. Keep stitching in this way until all the flowers and leaves are sewn on. Remove the pins as you sew.

8 If you want to add more stitching, blanket-stitch the edge of each flower and leaf to the blanket.

You can also use a fabric marker to draw swirly lines along the blanket edges. With an embroidery needle and six strands of floss or a chenille needle and yarn, backstitch (page 9) the lines.

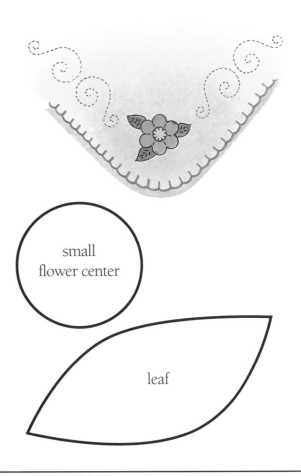

small flower center

leaf

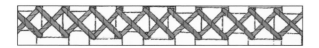

Cross-stitched ladybug magnet

Stick this whimsical bug on the fridge or your school locker. Use other patterns such as the heart, gecko or happy face (page 39), or a design of your own to make more magnets.

YOU WILL NEED

- a 13 cm (5 in.) square of 11-count Aida cloth
- a sewing needle and thread
- a small embroidery hoop
- red and black embroidery floss and a tapestry needle
- an 8 cm (3 in.) square of red or black felt
- stuffing (page 5)
- a small magnet with self-adhesive backing
- scissors, pins, a ruler, masking tape

HOW TO CROSS-STITCH

To prevent the Aida cloth from fraying, overcast-stitch (page 9) the edges with a sewing needle and thread, or bind them with masking tape.

To find the center of the Aida cloth, fold it in half and crease the fold with your fingernail. Unfold the fabric, then fold it in half the other way, crease it again and unfold it. Place it in the hoop (page 6) with the **+** where the creased lines cross at the center.

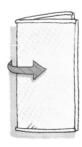
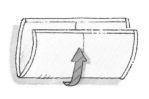

When you use a counted cross-stitch graph, one square on the graph represents one square on the fabric. Follow the top and side arrows on the graph to where they meet. This center point on the graph is the center of the cloth in the hoop.

Cross-stitch graphs are created with colors or symbols that represent different colors of embroidery floss so you know which ones to use.

The first diagonal stitch of each cross should be stitched from the bottom left corner to the upper right corner. The finishing cross-stitch in each square should always be stitched from the lower right to the upper left corner.

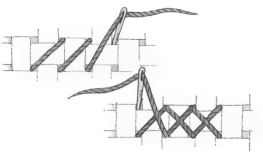

As you stitch, the strands of floss may untwist. Keep them twisted by turning the needle once or twice in a counterclockwise direction, every few stitches, as you pull the needle out of the fabric.

Keep your fabric smooth by pulling your stitches firmly but not too tightly.

When you finish each length of floss, weave in the ends (page 8) on the wrong side of the work. Make sure the ends don't get caught while you are stitching. Begin your second length of floss by weaving the needle back and forth once under a few stitches on the wrong side. When you are finished all the stitching, remove the masking tape, if you used it.

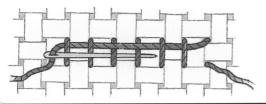

ladybug graph

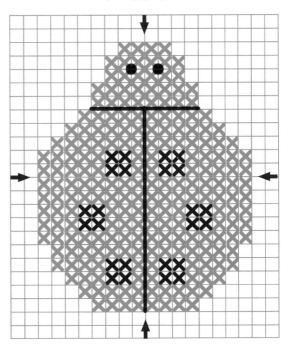

1 Place your Aida cloth in the hoop. Starting at the center, count ten squares up and two squares to the left. This is where you start stitching. With two strands of red embroidery floss, push the needle up through the bottom left hole of this square. Hold a 10 cm (4 in.) length of floss at the back for this step and the next so the first stitch doesn't pull out.

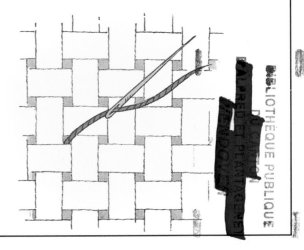

Instructions continue on the next page ☞

2 Push the needle down through the upper right hole of the same square.

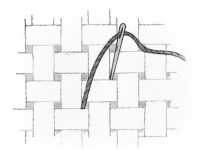

3 Push the needle up through the bottom right hole of the same square. Push the needle down through the upper right hole of the next square to the right. You should now have two diagonal stitches. Make two more to the right.

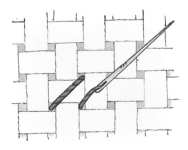

4 Stitch up through the bottom right hole and down through the top left hole of each square to finish or cross each stitch. You should now be back at the square where you started.

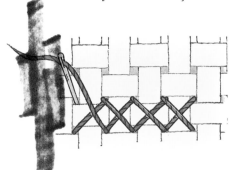

5 Following the graph (page 33), begin row 2, one square to the left and below row 1. Work from left to right to make six diagonal stitches, then cross them on your way back to the beginning of row 2.

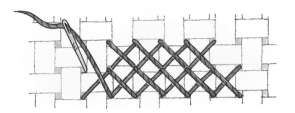

6 Following the graph, keep stitching in this way until all the red squares are stitched. (Starting at row 9, you will see a few black squares for the ladybug's spots. Leave these unstitched for now.)

7 With two strands of black floss, cross-stitch the black squares, then backstitch (page 9) the black lines below the head and down the center of the back.

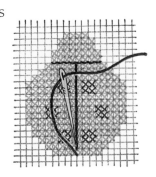

8 With two strands of black floss, French-knot (page 12) each eye.

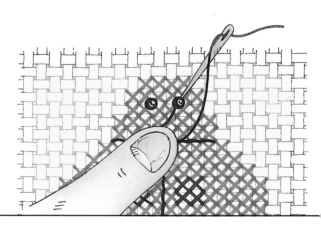

9 Remove the hoop. Place the ladybug, right side up, on a table. Center the felt square on top and pin it at each corner, then turn it over.

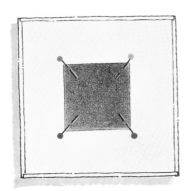

10 With a sewing needle and doubled, knotted thread, backstitch the Aida cloth to the felt all around the edge of the ladybug.

11 Cut out the ladybug, leaving 0.5 cm (1/4 in.) of fabric all around. With scissors, very carefully cut a slit down the center of the felt only.

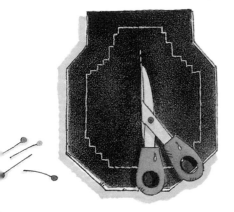

12 Turn the ladybug right side out and firmly stuff it. Overcast-stitch (page 9) the slit closed.

13 Stick the magnet over the seam.

14 With six strands of embroidery floss, push the needle in and out of the head where you want the two antennae. Remove the needle. On each end, tie an overhand knot close to the head, then again about 0.5 cm (1/4 in.) out. Trim each antenna just past the second knot.

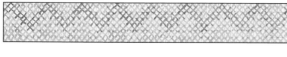

Bracelet

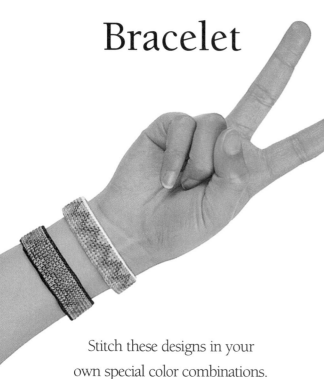

Stitch these designs in your
own special color combinations.

YOU WILL NEED

- a strip of 14-count Aida cloth about 20 cm x 4.5 cm (8 in. x 1¾ in.)
- a sewing needle and thread to match the Aida cloth
- a measuring tape
- a fabric marker (page 5)
- a large embroidery hoop
- embroidery floss and a tapestry needle
- a small button (optional)
- a 2.5 cm (1 in.) strip of Velcro (optional)
- a hot-glue gun (optional)
- a pencil, scissors, pins, masking tape (optional), an iron

1 Center the Aida cloth strip across the hoop (page 6).

2 To figure out how long your bracelet should be, measure around your wrist, then, with a fabric marker, mark thi length on the strip.

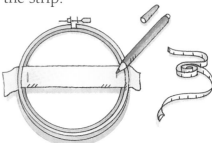

3 Cross-stitch (pages 32 and 33) a pattern along the center of this length

4 Remove the hoop. Ask an adult to help you fold under and press the short ends and one long edge, then fold under twice, press and pin the other long edge to the underside.

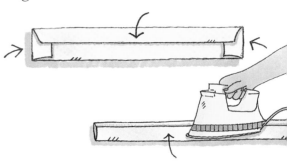

5 With a sewing needle and doubled, knotted thread, overcast-stitch (page 9) the pinned edge in place. Remove the pins as you sew.

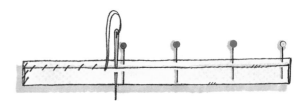

6 There are three ways to finish your bracelet: Velcro, ties or a button.

Ties: Cut six 25 cm (10 in.) lengths of three-strand embroidery floss. Thread a length into your needle, pull it halfway through one corner of the bracelet and remove the needle. Continue to attach a double length at each corner and in the center of each end. At each end, braid the three doubled lengths together and tie them together with an overhand knot.

Button: Stitch a loop of six-strand embroidery floss from corner to corner on one end of the bracelet and sew a small button on the top of the other end.

Velcro: You may need to trim the width of the Velcro to fit the bracelet width. Hot-glue (ask an adult to help) or backstitch (page 9) the hook side of the Velcro, hook side up, to the underside of the bracelet so it extends about 1.5 cm (5/8 in.) beyond one end. To the underside of the other end, glue or backstitch the other side of the Velcro, loop side down, even with the end.

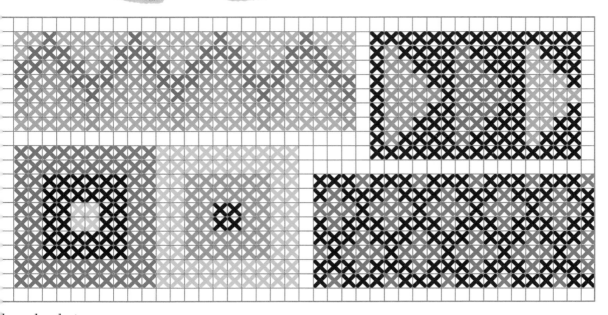

bracelet designs

Embroider on ...

Create your own cross-stitch or freehand designs to keep you in stitches. Be sure to add your name or initials and the date to your finished embroidery.

CROSS-STITCH

On graph paper, combine letters, numbers, motifs and borders
(pages 39 and 40) to make a design
with your name, a saying, a song, a prayer or a poem. You can also create your own cross-stitch patterns. Follow your graph to cross-stitch (pages 32
and 33) the design onto Aida cloth or any other even-weave fabric.

FREEHAND

Make a drawing of your pet, your friend or your family, or some flowers, the sun, the moon and stars — or whatever you like. Add rows of interesting stitches. When you are happy with your design, outline it in black permanent marker. Decide which stitches (pages 9 to 13) and colors you will use for different parts of your design and note them on the pattern. Draw or transfer (page 7) the pattern onto your choice of fabric or onto a
pillowcase or T-shirt.

You can make your embroidered fabric into one of the following projects:

- **Pillow**   From plain or printed fabric, cut a piece the same size as your embroidered fabric. With the right sides together and the edges even, pin the pieces of fabric along three edges. Backstitch (page 9) about 1 cm (½ in.) in from the pinned edges. Remove the pins as you sew. Turn the pillow cover right side out and ask an adult to help you fold under and press 1 cm (½ in.) around the unstitched edge. Slip in a pillow form or stuff with polyester fiber, then pin and overcast-stitch (page 9) the pressed edges together.

- **Table runner**   With a sewing needle and thread to match your fabric, overcast-stitch (page 9) the edges of the embroidered fabric. Ask an adult to help you fold under, press and pin 1 cm (½ in.) around the edges. With two strands of embroidery floss, use a running stitch (page 9) to sew the hem. Remove the pins as you sew.

• **Picture** Cut two pieces of corrugated cardboard, one piece of quilt batting and one piece of felt the size you want your finished picture to be. Glue together the two layers of cardboard. Center the quilt batting, then the embroidered fabric, right side up, on top of the cardboard. Turn everything over and tape, or ask an adult to help you hot-glue, the fabric edges to the back. Glue the felt to the back. Make a hanging loop by gluing or taping the ends of a ribbon to the top corners.

• You could also have your embroidery professionally framed.

No matter how you finish your embroidery, it may become an heirloom!

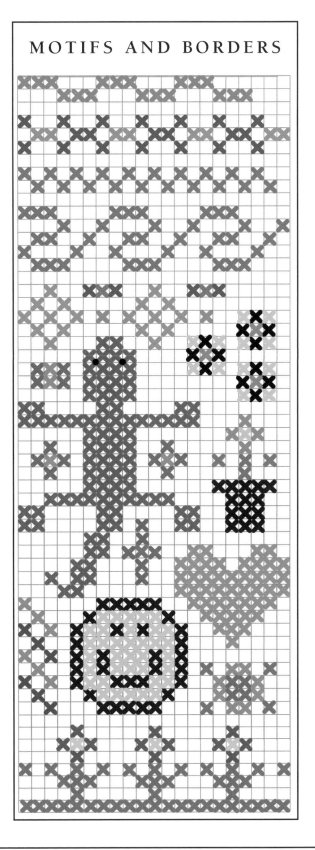

MOTIFS AND BORDERS